WORKBOOK FOR SOCIAL SKILLS TEENS NEED TO SURVIVE HIGH SCHOOL

PRACTICE ASSERTIVE COMMUNICATION WITH
BONUS CONTENT NOT INCLUDED IN THE TEXTBOOK

M. A. GALLANT

CONTENTS

Introduction — 5

1. STOP BEING PUSHED AROUND AND BECOME THE CEO OF YOUR LIFE — 7
   What Are Your Baseline Attitudes? — 7
   Let's Work on Body Language — 8

2. WHO ARE YOU, REALLY? — 13
   Start With Self-Reflection — 14
   Bonus Questions — 20
   Determining Your Personal Values — 24
   Reflection Questions — 27
   Define Your Personal Values — 29

3. YOU SET THE RULES — 31
   Your Personal Bill of Rights — 32
   Setting Boundaries — 32
   Understanding Your Emotions (Bonus Content) — 41
   Know What Your Boundaries Are and Use Them — 44
   Practice Saying "No" — 46

4. ASSERTIVENESS AT HOME — 49
   A Little Reflection First (Bonus) — 50
   Prepare and Practice for Future Conversations — 52
   Negotiations With Parents — 53
   Conversations With Parents (Bonus Practice) — 55
   Talking to Parents About Boundaries — 69

Conversations with Siblings 73
Conversations with Other Family
Members 87

5. WIN AT SCHOOL: TALKING TO
FRIENDS, TEACHERS, AND FOES 103
Friendship Evaluation Questions 103
Practicing Assertiveness With Friends 112
Dealing With Fake Friends (Frienemies) 115
Taking on the Bully 117
Interactions With Teachers 122

6. GETTING IT DONE AT YOUR JOB 125
Practice for the Interview 125
On the Job Communication Practice 134
Telling Your Boss "No" 139
When You Have No Choice but to Use the
"Hard No" 139
Situations Where You Could Say "Yes" but
You Don't Want To 141
Everyone's Favorite: Angry and Rude
Customers 143

7. ASSERTIVENESS AND DATING 149
Know How to Turn Down a Date 150
Dating and Boundaries 153
When Things Go Too Far 158

Conclusion 163
References 165

INTRODUCTION

I know that you eagerly want to change things in your life, such as being more comfortable standing up for yourself, and being able to say "no" to things you would rather not do. You want to express yourself, be heard, and be taken seriously. Learning to be assertive will give you this and more.

As with anything in life, practice is a part of learning. That is why this workbook is the perfect companion to "Social Skills Teens Need to Survive High School: Learn to communicate with Assertiveness to Spike Confidence, Gain Personal Growth and Squash Anxiety."

This workbook follows along with each chapter of the original book. It leads you deeper into each of the exercises and provides a place to write your answers to questions. It is a great place to keep a diary of your thoughts, feelings, and growth as you move through the book.

In this workbook, you will find not only each question and exercise from the book but also Bonus Features to take your practice to new levels that you won't find in the main book. You will get a deeper dive into the hands-on training from each chapter.

To best use this workbook, simply follow along as you move through each chapter. Whenever you see questions, come to the corresponding section here and fill in your responses. Complete each section of the workbook before moving on to the next section in the textbook.

By the time you finish both, you will feel more confident in your communication skills. You will have a better understanding of yourself. You will know how to tackle tough conversations. Best of all, this will add up to reduced anxiety related to social situations.

I wish you the best of luck on your journey.

You've got this!

Melissa Gallant

STOP BEING PUSHED AROUND AND BECOME THE CEO OF YOUR LIFE

WHAT ARE YOUR BASELINE ATTITUDES?

Let's begin by finding out where your attitudes about assertive communication are right now. Answer these few short questions and see how well they match up to the information in the book.

1. Give your definition of assertiveness

2. What attitudes do you have about assertive people?

3. How comfortable do you feel speaking your mind and standing up for yourself?

4. How committed are you to using this teaching to become more assertive?

LET'S WORK ON BODY LANGUAGE

Having good posture is a benefit to both your physical health and your mental health. That might sound odd, but when you stand up straight, with your shoulders back, and your head held high, something triggers a bolder attitude in your brain. It is hard to have low self-confidence in this stance. Even if you don't feel too sure of yourself at first, others will not pick up on it because your body is displaying confidence and comfort in the situation.

This exercise is straightforward. Simply see yourself right now, changing nothing about the way you carry yourself. Look at yourself in a mirror and consider how you look to yourself. Write all your thoughts and feelings about how you feel and see yourself.

Now, stand at attention. Straighten your back and hold your shoulders back. Look up, straight ahead. You may feel a bit rigid, so relax just slightly so that you are nice and upright, yet still physically comfortable.

Now look at yourself. Do you see the difference? If you usually slouch, you probably gained a few inches. How do you think a stranger would view you if they saw you right now? How much of a difference do you see in yourself? Write all your feelings about how you see yourself now.

Let's Go Deeper

Are your hands fidgeting? Do you stand with your arms crossed over your body? Are your feet and legs still or moving about?

Others may feel shut out when you cross your arms over your body. You want to appear open to conversation. Try to keep your arms to your side or allow them to move with your conversation to further express yourself positively. Sometimes it can be very hard to stand still, but all that movement makes you appear disengaged from the conversation.

For this exercise, spend some time practicing good posture and body language with your friends and family. Perhaps, say nothing about it, just let them see the transformation. See how many positive comments you get. Try this for a week and see how your feelings and attitudes change, as well as your interactions.

Write some notes about your experience.

Using Body Language a Little More Defensively

Let's think about situations of conflict. Starting with a friend who might be aggressive with their opinions or requests. Suppose you want to end the conversation.

In any situation where you would like to simply end the conversation, or when a person may be too close in your personal space, body language is here to help you.

You need to stand tall and use that good posture that you have been practicing. As you say, "no thank you" or "please step back a bit," or "I don't want to talk about this anymore," also place your hand out with fingers pointed up and palm facing the other person. This sends a clear message to "stop." If the situation has become heated, extend your arm out toward that person to drive your point further.

This may not be the right thing to do in all circumstances, especially where there is a threat of physical confrontation. If the threat of a physical fight is present, it is often best to just walk away from the situation.

Give this technique some practice. Ask a parent or friend to help you practice.

Write your thoughts, feelings, and experiences here.

2

WHO ARE YOU, REALLY?

As you are learning in the book, self-confidence is something that you can learn and improve. It starts with getting to know yourself better. It's important to understand yourself - both what you like and what you don't like - so that you can see what you want to change.

Self-reflection is a powerful tool that allows you to grow by understanding what makes you tick. You need to keep in mind, as with any tool, it must be used properly. What that means is that you need to be brutally honest with yourself when you go through these exercises.

Treat this workbook like a diary where you can express your deepest thoughts, even the ones you are not proud of. This is the only way for you to truly understand yourself and grow as a person.

START WITH SELF-REFLECTION

Answer the following questions from the main book. Remember to be as open and honest with yourself as possible.

1. How well do you handle your emotions when stressed? Do you scream or do you try to find a solution?

2. What thoughts do you have when you are going to sleep at night? Positive or negative?

3. Name 3 things or people that make you happy.

4. Name 5 things about yourself that you are comfortable with.

5. Name 5 things about yourself that you are uncomfortable with.

6. How would you change these 5 things if you could?

7. When was the last time you allowed someone to cross one of your boundaries?

8. What could you have done differently in the situation?

9. How do you show yourself respect?

10. In what ways do you go about working toward your goals? Are you a go-getter, or are you laid back and hoping it will just happen on its own?

11. What (or who) inspires you to get up in the morning and work toward your fullest potential?

12. Are you comfortable with the way your life is going right now? If not, why and how would you change it?

13. Where do you see yourself in 5 years?

14. 10 years?

15. 20 years?

16. Are the decisions you are making now going to make those dreams possible?

17. What are 5 adjectives you would use to describe yourself?

18. Ask 3 people how they would describe you and see how similar or different they are.

BONUS QUESTIONS

These questions help you better understand your answers to the previous questions. Answer the following to get a deeper idea of your thoughts and motivations.

1. Think about your answer to question #1. Picture the last time you felt stressed. How did you feel in that situation? Overwhelmed? Angry? Powerless? Express your feelings and emotions in that situation.

2. If you could relive that situation, how would you behave differently?

3. Next, referring to the prior question #2, on your thoughts while going to sleep. If those thoughts are positive, then great! You can skip to #7. This means that you are thinking positively and that is healthy for you. But if they are negative, write a few of those thoughts here.

4. Reflect on those negative thoughts that run through your head. How do they make you feel? What emotions do you relate to those thoughts?

5. Carefully examine those thoughts. Where do you think these thoughts come from?

6. If you see that these negative thoughts are not valid, then you need to work on the way you are "talking" to yourself. Start by trying to be aware of when these thoughts come up. When that happens, remind yourself that these are not valid. Redirect your thoughts to something that validates the actual truth. Think of 3 positive thoughts that you can replace the negative thoughts with. Practice this for a week. Then write your feelings about this exercise.

7. On the topic of 5 things about yourself that you are uncomfortable with. What can you do to move toward changing these things? Write one change action for every item you're listed.

8. Think about how you want your life to be in 5 years. Write 3 things that you can start working on now that will bring you closer to your goal. These can be short and long-term actions.

DETERMINING YOUR PERSONAL VALUES

Personal values are important because they guide your decision making. When people feel like they are living by their own values, they typically report being happier with themselves, have better self-esteem, and have less anxiety. This is because their actions align with their beliefs.

Answer the questions below to help you determine what your personal values are. These questions are the same as in the main book, but we added some bonus questions in.

1. Think of a time in your life when you felt happy with yourself. What were you doing?

2. Name two things that you are most proud of. Why do these make you feel proud?

3. Are you a leader or a follower? Write a few sentences supporting your answer and how you feel about your position.

4. Do you find it easy to forgive others when they hurt you?

5. Think of a time in your life when you felt satisfied and fulfilled. What were you doing? Who were you with?

6. Do you decide based on logic or emotion?

7. Do you solve problems using a plan or do you just go with your emotions?

8. How much effort are you willing to put in to achieve your goals?

9. What qualities do you admire in others?

10. Is it more important for you to be loved by all or respected by some? Explain why.

11. What kind of person do you want to be? Are you that person now?

REFLECTION QUESTIONS

Take some time to read over your answers to the Personal Values questions. Think about what your answers say about you and your core beliefs.

1. Are you happy with your answers? Why or why not?

2. What can you do to change any item that you are not happy with?

DEFINE YOUR PERSONAL VALUES

It can be hard to understand what "personal values" mean. My definition is *qualities that define what is important to you.* These are different for every person and influenced by things such as a person's relationships or career.

For example, I am a wife, mother, nurse, and author. Some of my personal values are loyalty, trust, compassion, dependability, maintaining health, and respect for personal choice.

The list of personal values of an Army General might also include loyalty and dependability, but they would place more value on things like bravery, leadership, and public safety.

Take some time to make a list of things that are important to you: your personal values. Start by choosing 10 values that are important to you. Use the chart in the main book if you need help.

Now, narrow that list to the 5 values that are most important to you right now. You can print it out and hang it up in your room or your locker at school to help you remember your values as the foundation for how you live your life.

3

YOU SET THE RULES

Now that you have read about personal rights, it's time for you to make your own Personal Bill of Rights.

Make a list of the rights you will establish for yourself. Remember, these are yours and you have the power to veto or amend this list as you see fit.

I encourage you to create a document with your list, personalize it anyway that you like, and display it in a prominent area of your space. Read it at the start of your day, every day, to keep yourself reminded of your own rights.

YOUR PERSONAL BILL OF RIGHTS

SETTING BOUNDARIES

Congratulations! You are making substantial progress toward becoming a more assertive person. Now that you have a good understanding of what your values are and you've established your Bill of Rights, it's time to take that information to set up the framework for the boundaries you will choose for yourself.

Answer the following questions honestly. This will help you understand what you want, and where you have vulnerabilities that need to be protected. The answers will help you establish boundaries that keep you safe, help you respect yourself and guide the decisions you make down the line. As a bonus, I added a few extra questions.

1. What characteristics do you think make up a healthy relationship?

2. Do all, some or few of your current relationships have these characteristics? Describe your answer.

3. Do you speak your mind in a conflict or agree to avoid conflict?

4. How often do you put the wants and needs of others before your own?

5. Do you think that is too much or not enough?

6. Is it hard for you to say "no" to people?

7. Do you feel guilty or afraid when you tell people "no"?

8. How often do you say "yes" to things you really don't want to do or be a part of?

9. Has this put you in a critical situation before? If so, describe it. If not, imagine a situation when being led down the wrong path by another could get you into trouble. Discuss what that might look like.

10. How do you respond when someone makes you feel uncomfortable?

11. What are some things people in your life now do that you are uncomfortable with?

12. Do you stand up for yourself when people mistreat you? How does that usually work out? If you don't stand up for yourself, then answer "why not"?

13. How many people can you honestly say you trust? Are you on that list?

14. Do you make it a priority to "fix" others' problems even if it has nothing to do with you? If so, why do you think you do this?

15. How often do you feel you are doing more than your share to keep a relationship going? How does this affect you emotionally?

16. Do you try to gain control over others? Do you allow others to control your life? Reflect on why you think this happens and if you should change it.

17. How often do you feel comfortable expressing your feelings, thoughts, and opinions with others, *regardless* of whether they are positive or negative?

18. How likely are you to end a relationship, platonic or romantic, if the other person keeps hurting or disrespecting you?

19. Have you ever used anger or intimidation to get your way? How so?

20. Have you ever had anyone use anger or intimidation against you? How did you handle it?

21. Do you think you could have done better? Write a better response.

22. How often do you allow yourself to be emotionally vulnerable (crying) in front of those you trust? Is this difficult for you?

23. Do you keep yourself emotionally distant from family and friends?

24. If being vulnerable is hard for you, try to think of why. Explore those thoughts below.

25. Are you often worried about what your friends, family and even parents think about you?

26. What thoughts do you think they have? Do you think they see the "real" you?

27. Do you feel guilty about wanting some alone time to relax?

28. Do you spend a large amount of time alone? If so, does this affect your relationships?

UNDERSTANDING YOUR EMOTIONS (BONUS CONTENT)

Understanding your emotions allows you to know yourself better, and it gives you the ability to express yourself in a more accurate way. Are you mad at a sibling? Of course, you know you are angry, but it is important to understand *why* you are angry. Emotions like anger and fear often have deeper underlying emotions, and those are the real ones to deal with.

Think of one recent situation in your life when you became angry. Write it down here.

Explore that anger. Describe the reason you became angry in as much detail as you can. Try to find the underlying emotions you felt, which you expressed as anger.

Often, we have deeper emotions that we don't recognize, and we express those feelings as anger. This is often the case if we feel things like rejection, fear, being misunderstood, or disrespect.

Were you able to find that underlying emotion in the previous exercise?

Use the space below to explore another example of a time when you reacted in anger and try to find the deeper underlying reason.

Now, think about your previous answer. How do you think it would have been different if you had expressed your deeper emotion rather than anger? Would you have been better understood? Would the conversation have gone in a better direction?

Next time you find yourself in an emotionally charged conversation, before you react, take a deep breath, and think about what you are really feeling (besides anger). Try calmly expressing your deeper emotion to the other person and see if the response is better.

KNOW WHAT YOUR BOUNDARIES ARE AND USE THEM

Now that you have explored some areas where you need to set boundaries and you have a better understanding of your emotions, it's time to put these skills into action. Write at least 5 boundaries that you want to establish right now. Then write some key phrases you will use to enforce these boundaries. If you need some help with coming up with key phrases, refer to Chapter 3, subheading *"How to Establish Boundaries."*

Boundary 1:

List 1-2 Key Phrases

Boundary 2:

List 1-2 Key Phrases

Boundary 3:

List 1-2 Key Phrases

Boundary 4:

List 1-2 Key Phrases

Boundary 5:

List 1-2 Key Phrases

PRACTICE SAYING "NO"

It would be impossible to behave assertively and truly communicate your thoughts, feelings, and emotions without ever using the word "no". You can't stand up for yourself and stop being a pushover without this powerful two-letter word.

It's time to practice using "no" in constructive ways. Use the space below to write 3 recent times that you agreed to something or said "yes" when you wanted to say "no". Write how you could use "no" respectfully and communicate your genuine desire. Try to find examples of using the "no, thank you", the "not now no" and the "hard no".

Example 1:

Example 2:

Example 3:

4

ASSERTIVENESS AT HOME

You've made it to the part where things get real and now you are ready to use assertive communication in your daily interactions. The safest place to practice is at home, where everyone loves and supports you. This is a good time to talk to your parents about your desire to become a more assertive person and ask for their support.

*Hint: If they know you are trying to practice, they may go easier on you when you are expressing yourself assertively, this might also be a time for a "big ask" *wink *wink!

A LITTLE REFLECTION FIRST (BONUS)

Before you jump right in, have a look at some recent conversations at home that didn't quite go your way. Take a minute to think of one or two, then answer the following questions:

Situation 1

Briefly describe what happened.

Think about how you expressed yourself and how you could have done better. Write your notes below:

Situation 2

Briefly describe what happened.

Think about how you could have expressed yourself better and write it below.

Situation 3

Briefly describe what happened.

Write how you could have done better.

PREPARE AND PRACTICE FOR FUTURE CONVERSATIONS

I am sure that like most teens; you have some things that you would like to see changed around your house. These issues could involve your parents, rules that you must follow, issues involving siblings, or issues that involve other family members.

If something comes to mind right now, use the questions below to prepare and practice for having this conversation. You can also save some or all of this area for future moments when you want to be prepared to have a mature conversation with someone in your family.

To make sure that you have plenty of room to practice and prepare, I have divided it into categories: parents, siblings, and other family members. Skip around and use each section when the time is right.

NEGOTIATIONS WITH PARENTS

Here are the 3 scenarios from the book. Use this as an exercise to improve your negotiation skills. Think about how you would best negotiate your request. Remember to gather evidence to support your case.

Scenario 1

How will you try to convince your parents to allow you to miss curfew to see a concert that is out of town?

Scenario 2

You want the new iPhone, and you have saved a lot of money already. How will you negotiate for a raise in your allowance so that you can get it as soon as they release it? What will you use to support your case? It might help if you find a way that this could benefit your parents, too.

Scenario 3

You want to get your nose pierced for your birthday. You know your parents are not a fan, but they allowed your older sibling to do the same at your age. Will you use this as part of your negotiation? It would be a good idea to find out why they are against it before using that strategy. What do you do?

CONVERSATIONS WITH PARENTS (BONUS PRACTICE)

The below blank scenarios are here for you to use as a place to practice situations from your real life. When a situation comes up, use this space to prepare for your conversations. You don't have to do this now. Wait for a time when it will really help you out.

Practice Scenario 1

What is the situation?

How do you feel about it? Remember to dig deep into the underlying feelings.

Quickly write the "gut reaction" you have.

[ ]

Now carefully think about an effective way to communicate your feelings, wishes, and need for the proposed change.

[ ]

Try to imagine how the other person will react and jot it down.

[ ]

Think of 1 or 2 negotiation points that you can make describing the benefits of the change, both for yourself and the other person.

When you are ready, find the right time and place for this conversation and go practice!

How did it go? Did you get what you wanted? Write thoughts on what went well, what went wrong, how you can improve next time.

Practice Scenario 2

What is the situation?

How do you feel about it? Remember to dig deep into the underlying feelings.

Quickly write the "gut reaction" you have.

Now carefully think about an effective way to communicate your feelings, wishes, and need for the proposed change.

Try to imagine how the other person will react and jot it down.

Think of 1 or 2 negotiation points that you can make describing the benefits of the change, both for yourself and the other person.

When you are ready, find the right time and place for this conversation and go practice!

How did it go? Did you get what you wanted? Write thoughts on what went well, what went wrong, how you can improve next time.

Practice Scenario 3

What is the situation?

How do you feel about it? Remember to dig deep into the underlying feelings.

Quickly write the "gut reaction" you have.

Now carefully think about an effective way to communicate your feelings, wishes, and need for the proposed change.

Try to imagine how the other person will react and jot it down.

Think of 1 or 2 negotiation points that you can make describing the benefits of the change, both for yourself and the other person.

When you are ready, find the right time and place for this conversation and go practice!

How did it go? Did you get what you wanted? Write thoughts on what went well, what went wrong, how you can improve next time.

Practice Scenario 4

What is the situation?

How do you feel about it? Remember to dig deep into the underlying feelings.

Quickly write the "gut reaction" you have.

Now carefully think about an effective way to communicate your feelings, wishes, and need for the proposed change.

Try to imagine how the other person will react and jot it down.

Think of 1 or 2 negotiation points that you can make describing the benefits of the change, both for yourself and the other person.

When you are ready, find the right time and place for this conversation and go practice!

How did it go? Did you get what you wanted? Write thoughts on what went well, what went wrong, how you can improve next time.

Practice Scenario 5

What is the situation?

How do you feel about it? Remember to dig deep into the underlying feelings.

Quickly write the "gut reaction" you have.

Now carefully think about an effective way to communicate your feelings, wishes, and need for the proposed change.

Try to imagine how the other person will react and jot it down.

Think of 1 or 2 negotiation points that you can make describing the benefits of the change, both for yourself and the other person.

When you are ready, find the right time and place for this conversation and go practice!

How did it go? Did you get what you wanted? Write thoughts on what went well, what went wrong, how you can improve next time.

TALKING TO PARENTS ABOUT BOUNDARIES

The book has some common boundary issues that arise between parents and teens. When trying to set boundaries with your parents, it is best to keep in mind that they have final say. The only thing you can do at this point is to state your case maturely, respectfully, and express yourself as honestly as you can. Doing this will help them realize how crossing your personal boundaries affects you, and you may find that they respect your approach and change their behavior.

Before having these conversations with your parents, take time to think about and plan your approach. Use the spaces below to prepare.

Scenario 1

Your parent looked through your room when you were not around. How do you best express how this makes you feel while being respectful and ask them to stop doing this?

Scenario 2

Your parents expect you to babysit your younger sibling every weekend and now that you are older, you would like more freedom on the weekends. Again, how do you express yourself to produce a constructive conversation with your parents?

Use the space below to practice other boundary situations that may come up between you and your parents.

Scenario:

How do you communicate?

Scenario:

How do you communicate?

CONVERSATIONS WITH SIBLINGS

A million different situations can come up between siblings with boundary setting. Use what you have learned so far to practice how you would set boundaries with your siblings.

(If you don't have siblings, you can use this space for any situation that you may need to practice.)

Practice Scenario 1

What is the situation?

How do you feel about it? Remember to dig deep into the underlying feelings.

Quickly write the "gut reaction" you have.

Now carefully think about an effective way to communicate your feelings, wishes, and need for the proposed change.

Try to imagine how the other person will react and jot it down.

Think of 1 or 2 negotiation points that you can make describing the benefits of the change, both for yourself and the other person.

When you are ready, find the right time and place for this conversation and go practice!

How did it go? Did you get what you wanted? Write thoughts on what went well, what went wrong, how you can improve next time.

Practice Scenario 2

What is the situation?

How do you feel about it? Remember to dig deep into the underlying feelings.

Quickly write the "gut reaction" you have.

Now carefully think about an effective way to communicate your feelings, wishes, and need for the proposed change.

Try to imagine how the other person will react and jot it down.

Think of 1 or 2 negotiation points that you can make describing the benefits of the change, both for yourself and the other person.

When you are ready, find the right time and place for this conversation and go practice!

How did it go? Did you get what you wanted? Write thoughts on what went well, what went wrong, how you can improve next time.

Practice Scenario 3

What is the situation?

How do you feel about it? Remember to dig deep into the underlying feelings.

Quickly write the "gut reaction" you have.

Now carefully think about an effective way to communicate your feelings, wishes, and need for the proposed change.

Try to imagine how the other person will react and jot it down.

Think of 1 or 2 negotiation points that you can make describing the benefits of the change, both for yourself and the other person.

When you are ready, find the right time and place for this conversation and go practice!

How did it go? Did you get what you wanted? Write thoughts on what went well, what went wrong, how you can improve next time.

Practice Scenario 4

What is the situation?

How do you feel about it? Remember to dig deep into the underlying feelings.

Quickly write the "gut reaction" you have.

Now carefully think about an effective way to communicate your feelings, wishes, and need for the proposed change.

Try to imagine how the other person will react and jot it down.

Think of 1 or 2 negotiation points that you can make describing the benefits of the change, both for yourself and the other person.

When you are ready, find the right time and place for this conversation and go practice!

How did it go? Did you get what you wanted? Write thoughts on what went well, what went wrong, how you can improve next time.

Practice Scenario 5

What is the situation?

How do you feel about it? Remember to dig deep into the underlying feelings.

Quickly write the "gut reaction" you have.

Now carefully think about an effective way to communicate your feelings, wishes, and need for the proposed change.

Try to imagine how the other person will react and jot it down.

Think of 1 or 2 negotiation points that you can make describing the benefits of the change, both for yourself and the other person.

When you are ready, find the right time and place for this conversation and go practice!

How did it go? Did you get what you wanted? Write thoughts on what went well, what went wrong, how you can improve next time.

CONVERSATIONS WITH OTHER FAMILY MEMBERS

What types of situations with more distant family members could use some assertiveness and boundary setting? Practice those situations here, and you can be prepared for the next family reunion.

Practice Scenario 1

What is the situation?

How do you feel about it? Remember to dig deep into the underlying feelings.

Quickly write the "gut reaction" you have.

Now carefully think about an effective way to communicate your feelings, wishes, and need for the proposed change.

Try to imagine how the other person will react and jot it down.

Think of 1 or 2 negotiation points that you can make describing the benefits of the change, both for yourself and the other person.

When you are ready, find the right time and place for this conversation and go practice!

How did it go? Did you get what you wanted? Write thoughts on what went well, what went wrong, how you can improve next time.

Practice Scenario 2

What is the situation?

How do you feel about it? Remember to dig deep into the underlying feelings.

Quickly write the "gut reaction" you have.

Now carefully think about an effective way to communicate your feelings, wishes, and need for the proposed change.

Try to imagine how the other person will react and jot it down.

Think of 1 or 2 negotiation points that you can make describing the benefits of the change, both for yourself and the other person.

When you are ready, find the right time and place for this conversation and go practice!

How did it go? Did you get what you wanted? Write thoughts on what went well, what went wrong, how you can improve next time.

Practice Scenario 3

What is the situation?

How do you feel about it? Remember to dig deep into the underlying feelings.

Quickly write the "gut reaction" you have.

Now carefully think about an effective way to communicate your feelings, wishes, and need for the proposed change.

Try to imagine how the other person will react and jot it down.

Think of 1 or 2 negotiation points that you can make describing the benefits of the change, both for yourself and the other person.

When you are ready, find the right time and place for this conversation and go practice!

How did it go? Did you get what you wanted? Write thoughts on what went well, what went wrong, how you can improve next time.

Practice Scenario 4

What is the situation?

How do you feel about it? Remember to dig deep into the underlying feelings.

Quickly write the "gut reaction" you have.

Now carefully think about an effective way to communicate your feelings, wishes, and need for the proposed change.

Try to imagine how the other person will react and jot it down.

Think of 1 or 2 negotiation points that you can make describing the benefits of the change, both for yourself and the other person.

When you are ready, find the right time and place for this conversation and go practice!

How did it go? Did you get what you wanted? Write thoughts on what went well, what went wrong, how you can improve next time.

Practice Scenario 5

What is the situation?

How do you feel about it? Remember to dig deep into the underlying feelings.

Quickly write the "gut reaction" you have.

Now carefully think about an effective way to communicate your feelings, wishes, and need for the proposed change.

Try to imagine how the other person will react and jot it down.

Think of 1 or 2 negotiation points that you can make describing the benefits of the change, both for yourself and the other person.

When you are ready, find the right time and place for this conversation and go practice!

How did it go? Did you get what you wanted? Write thoughts on what went well, what went wrong, how you can improve next time.

5

WIN AT SCHOOL: TALKING TO FRIENDS, TEACHERS, AND FOES

In your teen years, school and social life are a huge part of who you are. If you've heard the phrase, "You are those who you spend the most time with," then you may realize that there will be times when you must evaluate your friendships. If you question whether to continue a relationship with one of your peers, here are some questions to help you out.

FRIENDSHIP EVALUATION QUESTIONS

Person 1

1. Does this person support you?

2. Does this person respect your boundaries?

3. Can you trust this person?

4. Do they make you feel good or bad about yourself?

5. Do they have characteristics that support your personal values?

6. How do you feel when you are around them?

7. Do they take part in activities that you do not approve of?

8. How do they treat other people?

9. How do your family members feel about them?

10. How do your other friends feel about them?

11. List qualities that make you want to continue the relationship.

12. List qualities that make you want to end the relationship.

Read over all your prior questions, reflect on them for a while, and then write your final thoughts.

Person 2

1. Does this person support you?

2. Does this person respect your boundaries?

3. Can you trust this person?

4. Do they make you feel good or bad about yourself?

5. Do they have characteristics that support your personal values?

6. How do you feel when you are around them?

7. Do they take part in activities that you do not approve of?

8. How do they treat other people?

9. How do your family members feel about them?

10. How do your other friends feel about them?

11. List qualities that make you want to continue the relationship.

12. List qualities that make you want to end the relationship.

Read over all your prior questions, reflect on them for a while, and then write your final thoughts.

Person 3

1. Does this person support you?

2. Does this person respect your boundaries?

3. Can you trust this person?

4. Do they make you feel good or bad about yourself?

5. Do they have characteristics that support your personal values?

6. How do you feel when you are around them?

7. Do they take part in activities that you do not approve of?

8. How do they treat other people?

9. How do your family members feel about them?

10. How do your other friends feel about them?

11. List qualities that make you want to continue the relationship.

12. List qualities that make you want to end the relationship.

Read over all your prior questions, reflect on them for a while, and then write your final thoughts.

PRACTICING ASSERTIVENESS WITH FRIENDS

High school is a time filled with conflict, even with your best friends. You are going to find yourself in some hairy situations and it is best to be prepared. The following exercises let you have answers to hard questions ready so that you can use them when you need to.

How would you respond if a friend suggests the following? (Bonus)

1. I know you are really nervous about this test. Why don't you take one of my Adderall to help you calm down and focus?

2. Let's go to the bonfire out in the woods. Everyone is going to be there, and they are going to have a keg!

3. I snagged some smokes out of my dad's pack. Let's sneak off somewhere and smoke.

4. Just pour some of this vodka into your Coke bottle, no one will even know!

5. I don't want to go to school today, let's just skip.

6. We could sneak out of your window so easily! Your parents will never even know we left!

DEALING WITH FAKE FRIENDS (FRIENEMIES)

As mentioned in the book, here are the Fake Friend Scenarios from chapter 5. Write how you would respond to these situations in your own words.

Scenario 1

Someone in your circle of friends is picking on you, making fun of you, or gossiping about you. Your closer friends are not saying anything about it. What do you say?

Scenario 2

Your friend is touching you in a way that does not respect your boundaries. (Playfully punching your arm, scuffing your hair, planting a big kiss on your cheek) How do you respond?

Scenario 3

Your friend has been in a bad mood and has been very argumentative. You feel like they are having personal issues, and you want to help, but you're tired of the constant combativeness. How do you respond?

TAKING ON THE BULLY

Scenario 1

Someone who has been bullying you in the hallways at school finally pushes you to take action. What do you do?

Scenario 2

Someone is harassing you by using social media to humiliate you. Do you confront them or seek help from a parent or school official?

Scenario 3

What would you say if someone challenged you to a fight? How would you avoid the fight?

Scenario 4

Someone that you don't even know is sending harassing messages on a social media or gaming platform. First, how does it make you feel? Do you take the words personally? If you do, you shouldn't. Do you engage with them? Do you block them?

Bonus Section: Reflection on Bullies

When taking some of these scenarios into consideration, spend some time reflecting on how these things affect you mentally. Answer the following questions honestly and then reflect on your answers for insight into your thought process.

1. How often do you take ugly comments from someone else personally?

2. Do you believe that there is any truth in what that person is saying?

3. Do negative things that are said, whether in real life or online, make you feel bad about yourself?

4. How much time do you spend thinking about the negative comments others say about you?

5. Do you think that negative behavior directed toward you says more about you or the other person?

Hopefully, you see that these things often are not based on truth at all. Being able to realize that when someone is acting like a bully or being mean for no apparent reason, it has more to do with that person's personal and mental issues than it does you.

Understandably, it's easy to feel hurt when someone is mistreating you, but how you choose to allow it to affect you is very important. Being self-aware allows you to choose not to let these things affect your self-esteem and mental health. Try to take your feelings out of the situation and examine if the words or actions are valid. I am sure if you think about it with logic instead of emotion, you will find that they are not true or valid.

Use this space to write your thoughts and feelings about this.

INTERACTIONS WITH TEACHERS

Your teachers can be great allies when you need them for things like extra help in a class that you are struggling in or getting a great recommendation to the college you want to apply to.

Teachers are humans too, and they have bad days, just like the rest of us. How would you respond to the following scenarios?

Scenario 1

You got a poor grade that you did not expect. You should talk to your teacher about it. It is possible that you did not understand the expectations of the work, but it is also possible that your teacher will see your side of the situation, and if you communicate properly, you could get an improved grade.

How do you start the conversation? Write it here in your own words.

Scenario 2

Your teacher accused you of something you didn't do. The example was cheating on a test. However, this can be applied to any situation where you are falsely accused.

Think of a situation and write down how you would handle it when talking to your teacher, or even your principal.

6

GETTING IT DONE AT YOUR JOB

Getting your first job can be quite intimidating, especially if you are not prepared. Luckily, you are learning how to ace the interview. Just like everything else, preparation is the key.

Remember, you want to express yourself as someone who really wants the job, a person who is mature and responsible, and someone with a pleasant personality who the owner or manager will want representing their business.

PRACTICE FOR THE INTERVIEW

(You can save this section for when you are applying for a real job.)

Be ready to ace the interview by answering the following questions. One key way to put your best foot forward is to customize your responses to the job you are trying to get. Check the company's website and find out what they are all about.

Do they promise stellar customer service? Express your desire to be a customer service expert.

Maybe offering the highest quality product is important to them. Communicate how you will work hard to provide the best quality when working there.

Chances are good that you will apply for several jobs while in high school. I am giving you space to prepare for three different jobs.

When you are done, read back over your answers. Make sure that you are happy with your responses and then practice them before your interview. Have a friend or parent practice with you. It's best to practice answering out loud, not just in your head.

Interview Questions Job 1

1. Why do you want to work here?

2. Can you tell me a little about yourself?

3. Can you work on weekends?

4. What are some of your strengths and weaknesses?

5. Do you have reliable transportation?

6. If we are short staffed, would you be able to come to work on short notice?

7. What position are you most interested in?

8. What do you think you will like about working here?

9. What do you think you will not like about working here?

10. Tell me why I should hire you.

Interview Questions Job 2

1. Why do you want to work here?

2. Can you tell me a little about yourself?

3. Can you work on weekends?

4. What are some of your strengths and weaknesses?

5. Do you have reliable transportation?

6. If we are short staffed, would you be able to come to work on short notice?

7. What position are you most interested in?

8. What do you think you will like about working here?

9. What do you think you will not like about working here?

10. Tell me why I should hire you.

Interview Questions Job 3

1. Why do you want to work here?

2. Can you tell me a little about yourself?

3. Can you work on weekends?

4. What are some of your strengths and weaknesses?

5. Do you have reliable transportation?

6. If we are short staffed, would you be able to come to work on short notice?

7. What position are you most interested in?

8. What do you think you will like about working here?

9. What do you think you will not like about working here?

10. Tell me why I should hire you.

ON THE JOB COMMUNICATION PRACTICE

Below, you will find scenarios from the book. Practice how you can best handle the following situations.

Scenario 1

You have made a mistake. Your boss noticed and is now talking to you about it. In this practice, you are clearly in the wrong and need to take responsibility and show willingness to improve. Think of a couple of situations that might happen at your job and practice the best way to respond.

Situation 1:

Your best response:

Situation 2:

Your best response:

Situation 3:

Your best response:

Scenario 2

The scenario in the book involved dealing with a money mix up. However, there are many examples of how a simple mistake can look like something far worse, and your boss will surely want to understand it.

If this ever happens to you, the first thing to remember is to stay calm. Take a couple of deep breaths to help you avoid panic and think straight.

Consider some examples that might happen and practice how you should respond.

Example 1: missing money

What could happen:

[   ]

How would best explain the situation to your boss so that they don't accuse you of stealing?

[   ]

Example 2: a customer falsely accuses you of giving back the wrong change

What could happen:

[   ]

How would you best communicate with your boss that you did nothing wrong? What suggestion would you make to resolve this situation?

Example 3 (bonus): You are accused you of not showing up for a shift that you were not scheduled for.

What could happen:

How would you communicate with your boss that you are not in the wrong? What evidence could you provide?

TELLING YOUR BOSS "NO"

In the working world, it is common to need to tell the boss "no." I know that I have faced many of these situations. How you communicate will influence your relationship with your boss and possibly even how long you will work there.

From the boss's point of view, they have a company to run. It is their responsibility to keep it running efficiently and to get the job done. They may also have a boss of their own to answer to.

These things are not your responsibility, especially if they are asking you to do something that you legally may not do, or if they are taking advantage of you.

Use the following scenario examples to practice saying "no" to your boss. You may even want to practice some of these with a parent or friend.

WHEN YOU HAVE NO CHOICE BUT TO USE THE "HARD NO"

Scenario 1

Your boss has asked you to work later than you are allowed to according to the laws of your state (which you should be familiar with when you begin working).

How do you respond?

Scenario 2 (bonus)

Your boss asks you to sell tobacco or alcohol and you are not old enough to do so legally. (Do you know that *you* can be charged a huge fine if you do this?)

How do you respond?

Scenario 3 (bonus)

Your boss asks you to make a delivery, but you only have a learner's permit and are not allowed to drive a car alone yet.

How do you respond?

SITUATIONS WHERE YOU COULD SAY "YES" BUT YOU DON'T WANT TO

Bonus Section

Sometimes, you have no choice but to refuse the boss's request, but there will also be times when you have the option of saying "yes" but you prefer to say "no."

Your boss may try to pressure you - remember, they have a responsibility to get the job done, and that is why they are making the request. That doesn't mean that you must give in to appease them. It means that you need to be assertive and not allow them to take advantage of you.

Think of some ways that you might respond to the following situations.

Scenario 1:

Your boss has asked you to work on a day that you have already requested off, and that request was approved.

How can you best say "no" to this request?

Scenario 2:

Your shift is almost over, and your friends are waiting for you to clock out because you have made plans. At the last minute, your boss asks if you can stay a couple of hours late.

Supposing that you do not want the extra work hours, how do you respond?

Scenario 3:

This one is different, but it can happen.

Suppose you have been working, and you love your job. Your boss has noticed, and they offer you a promotion to Shift Leader.

You may have several reasons for not wanting to take the promotion, such as not wanting more responsibility or not wanting to be in charge.

How do you respectfully turn the offer down? Remember, thank your boss for considering you. It is a compliment, after all.

EVERYONE'S FAVORITE: ANGRY AND RUDE CUSTOMERS

Dealing with angry and rude customers is by far the hardest part of any job, especially those in which you will deal with the public. This applies to most teens because common jobs for teens are in restaurants, grocery stores, coffee shops, and retail stores. Even if your high school job is mowing lawns, you will still have to deal with customers.

The best way to deal with any angry person is to remain calm and use assertive communication.

Let's Practice the Scenarios from the Book, plus a bonus.

Just like before, practice responding in your own words.

Scenario 1

A customer is angry that their order is not correct, or their food is cold. They demand to have a full refund and new food prepared. This is against your company's policy.

How do you respond?

Scenario 2

You have a very impatient customer who has been making loud comments while waiting in line. They have been unhappy with having to wait, but the situation was unavoidable.

What are some things you can do and say that will help to diffuse the situation? Remember, body language is an important tool.

Scenario 3

You are working the customer service counter and a customer would like to return an item that does not fall into the parameters for a refund.

How do you explain this to the customer?

Scenario 4 (Bonus)

You are a hostess at a nice restaurant. There is a crowd of people waiting to be seated. Suddenly, a man approaches you. He is furious, and he is aggressively pointing his finger at you and shouting, "Get me the manager right now! I am so pissed off! My food is all wrong and I demand to talk to your boss NOW!" The man is right in your face and his pointed finger is inches from your nose.

Remembering body language and assertive communication. How do you handle this? (No cheating by reading ahead!)

Ok, I admit, that one may have been a curveball, because we did not address this type of aggressive customer in the book.

How does your answer compare to this?

You stand up straight, pull your shoulders back, and you take 1 step backwards while putting your hand up with your arm extended.

Then you could say, "Sir, I can see that you are upset. I want to help you, but please calm down and lower your voice."

(Assuming he does so)

Then say, "I want to help you. Please fully explain what happened so that I can let my manager know, and I will get them right away."

How did you do?

How would you feel in this situation? I am sure that it would be scary, but that shouldn't stop you from standing up for yourself and taking control of the situation.

ASSERTIVENESS AND DATING

Dating is a big part of life for most teens. It is a time when everything feels extreme - having a crush on someone can feel exciting and if you date that person, you can have all kinds of tingling emotions running amuck in your head and heart.

Dating can also cause a lot of conflict. This can be between you and your romantic partner or between you and your friends. You may have to deal with jealousy on all fronts. These are just some reasons that all teens should learn to be assertive.

KNOW HOW TO TURN DOWN A DATE

With dating being such a popular issue in high school, it might seem like everyone is looking for someone to pair up with. Whether or not you are interested in dating, you will have some people who want to date you that you aren't interested in, and vice versa.

I'm sure that if you want to turn down a date offer, you want to do it as nicely as possible without being hurtful to the other person. It's a good time to practice saying "no" with kindness.

Scenario 1

Someone that you consider a close friend expresses romantic feelings to you and asks you for a date. You don't think of this person in that way, and you want to let them down without hurting them or your friendship.

Write your best response. Remember to be kind, but honest about your feelings and what you want.

Scenario 2

In this situation, you are dating someone, and another classmate asks you out on a date. How would you say "no" directly that is not hurtful to the other person?

Bonus Scenario

This situation is a little tricky. I have included it because it happened to me when I was your age.

Suppose one of your parents has a friend who also has teen about the same age as you. The parents arrange an outing to include the 4 of you. Let's just say that it was a trip to the zoo.

While there, the other teen catches a moment while the parents are out of earshot and says, "My mom brought me here to meet you because she thought it would be nice if we went out. I guess our moms think that would be fun for them."

What would your first thoughts and gut reaction be?

I would not be surprised if you said something about being a little angry with your parent. Let's continue, with the scenario and the other teen saying, "I wasn't sure, but now that we've met, I would like to go on a date with you, you know, without the Moms tagging along."

Let's assume that you are not interested in dating this person. How do you feel about being put in this situation, and how do you respond to the request for a date?

Would you feel differently if it had been a friend who set you up instead of your parent?

DATING AND BOUNDARIES

Dating is a time when personal boundaries are of the utmost of importance. Making your boundaries known will hopefully save you a lot of grief. Remember that the boundaries you set are a way of respecting yourself. So, allowing the person you are dating to cross those boundaries is you letting yourself down.

Let's explore the scenarios in the book.

Scenario 1

The person you are dating is jealous, even of your friends and family. They try to control you by constantly texting, calling and showing up when they were not invited or welcome.

How would you feel if this happened to you?

Would you want to continue the relationship? Answer below and explain why - regardless of whether you said "yes" or "no".

Based on your answer above, what would you do and say? Remember to include body language in your answer.

If you ever find yourself in a situation like this one, it is best to talk to your parents about it, especially if the situation escalates. Remember, parents are always on your side and will help to keep you safe.

Scenario 2

Public Displays of Affection (PDA) - something that you may very well be uncomfortable with and something that can very well get you in trouble, especially at school. It is best to set boundaries like this early in the relationship so that everyone agrees.

Imagine that you have just started dating someone who seems to crave PDA all the time. How would you set your boundaries early in the relationship?

What would you do if the behavior continued? Would you offer a second chance, or end the relationship?

Write your response below with how you would assertively express yourself.

Scenario 3

The person you are dating has become bossy, even telling you how they want you to dress and act.

How would this make you feel?

How would you express yourself to them about this behavior?

What would you do if the behavior persisted?

Scenario 4

At any age, it's easy to get caught up in a relationship and allow it to consume a lot of your time. In this scenario, your partner is not at fault, but you realize you need to focus more attention on your friends and family, as well as schoolwork.

How would you talk to your partner about this?

How might you respond if that person had a negative reaction and became upset?

WHEN THINGS GO TOO FAR

The topic of sexual intimacy may be uncomfortable for many people, especially teens. I feel it would be irresponsible not to include it in a book that is about boundary setting and assertiveness.

It is important for anyone of any age to be prepared to deal with this topic if they are in a romantic relationship.

To help you be prepared, consider the following situations that will happen to you at some point (if they haven't already).

Scenario 1

The person who you are dating wants to have sex, but you are not ready. Let's first assume that the relationship is new, and this is the first time the topic has come up.

How do you assert yourself and set your boundaries?

Now, let's advance the timeline a few weeks. How would you affirm your boundaries?

Let's imagine that the relationship with this same person has continued for a year. You have not changed your position about sexual activity, but now they are putting more and more pressure on you to do so. They are even using guilt as a weapon to change your mind.

Write about your feelings.

How would you have an assertive conversation with them while sticking to your boundaries? Do you think you would want to continue or end the relationship? Write your thoughts and feelings about this.

What would that conversation be like?

Scenario 2

No matter how many times you have said "yes" to any situation does not mean that you are stuck with that decision. "Yes" does not void any future "no".

Remember that you decide when, how often, how many times you do anything. This scenario is about sex, but it could also apply to drinking alcohol, smoking, cheating on a test, sneaking out of the house, and any other situation that might arise.

Consider the scenario from the book. You have engaged in some sexual acts with your partner, but you have decided that you do not want to do it anymore. This is your right and the reason for this change does not matter, though including the reason may help the conversation go better.

Imagine that you are in this situation and write about how you would talk to your partner about it.

Write your answer below.

CONCLUSION

Throughout this workbook, you have honed your assertive communication skills. By now, you should have done some self-reflection to discover what you love and what you want to improve about yourself. You should have a Personal Bill of Rights and a list of Personal Boundaries. You should have a good idea of what your most important values are. I hope you review these often so that you don't lose sight of what you are working toward.

You should also have many assertive conversations under your belt by now. I hope you continue to practice this new skill. Assertive people report higher self-esteem, less anxiety and they get what they want out of life. This is because they take an active role in controlling their life. Though you may not be a pro yet, keep working on it - it will only benefit you!

I hope you found this workbook to be very helpful. If so, I would really appreciate it if you left an honest review on Amazon. Your review will help me assist more high school students just like you.

www.EtheriaPublishing/Reviews/AssertivenessWorkbook

REFERENCES

Ackerman, C. E. (2017, December 18). *87 Self-Reflection Questions for Introspection*. Positive Psychology. https://positivepsychology.com/introspection-self-reflection/

Assertive Communication—6 Tips for Effective Use. (n.d.). Impact Factory. https://www.impactfactory.com/resources/assertive-communication-6-tips-for-effective-use/

Assertiveness. (2019). Psychology Today. https://www.psychologytoday.com/us/basics/assertiveness

Baird, A. (2017, August 14). *Assertive Body Language*. Sensei. https://sensei.ie/assertive-body-language/

Barkley, S., & Currin-Sheehan, K. (2022, September 15). *This is How to Set Boundaries With Your Parents*. Psych Central. https://psychcentral.com/relationships/setting-boundaries-with-parents#parental-boundaries-are-unique

Dani. (2021, August 19). *The Importance of Self-Reflection as a Teenager in 2022*. Teen Financial Freedom. https://teenfinancialfreedom.com/the-importance-of-self-reflection-as-a-teenager-in-2022/

Darcy, A. M. (2019, June 25). *12 Signs You Lack Healthy Boundaries (and Why You Need Them)*. Harley Therapy™ Blog. https://www.harleytherapy.co.uk/counselling/healthy-boundaries.htm

Five Steps to Negotiating With Parents and Carers. (n.d.). Young Scot. https://young.scot/get-informed/national/five-steps-to-negotiating-with-parents-and-carers

Gordon, S. (2021, July 26). *Everything Your Teen Needs to Know About Setting Boundaries*. Verywell Family. https://www.verywellfamily.com/boundaries-what-every-teen-needs-to-know-5119428

Gordon, S. (2022, March 7). *7 Ways to Improve Assertiveness So You Don't Get Bullied*. Verywell Family. https://www.verywellfamily.com/how-teaching-assertiveness-can-prevent-bullying-460681

Healthwise. (2017, October 10). *Stress Management: Reducing Stress by Being Assertive*. Kaiser Permanente. https://wa.kaiserpermanente.org/kbase/topic.jhtml?docId=av2095

How to Deal With Annoying, Difficult, and Disrespectful Siblings. (2019, November 25). UpJourney. https://upjourney.com/how-to-deal-with-annoying-difficult-and-disrespectful-siblings

The Importance of Knowing & Living Your Values. (2020, July 1). Applied Positive Psychology Learning Institute. https://appli.edu.au/knowing-living-your-values/

Jay, C. (2022, September 11). *How to Refuse a Date Gracefully: 12 steps*. WikiHow. https://www.wikihow.com/Refuse-a-Date-Gracefully

Konter-O'Hara, S. (2022, September 23). *Personal Boundaries Quiz*. WellMinded Counseling. https://wellmindedcounseling.com/therapist-blog/2016/9/5/personal-boundaries-quiz

McGregor, J. (2017, May 29). *How to Be Assertive and Set Healthy Boundaries*. Welldoing. https://welldoing.org/article/how-be-assertive-set-healthy-boundaries

Mizrahi, J. (2020, April 27). *The Importance of Self-Reflection in Learning*. Today's Learner. https://todayslearner.cengage.com/the-importance-of-self-reflection-in-learning

Panayotova, L. (2015, December 22). *Personal Bill of Rights*. Explorable. https://explorable.com/e/personal-bill-of-rights

Self-Reflection 101: What Is Self-Reflection? Why Is Reflection Important? And How to Reflect. (2020). Holstee. https://www.holstee.com/blogs/mindful-matter/self-reflection-101-what-is-self-reflection-why-is-reflection-important-and-how-to-reflect

Stressed Out? Be Assertive. (2022, May 13). Mayo Clinic. https://www.mayoclinic.org/healthy-lifestyle/stress-management/in-depth/assertive/art-20044644

Teaching Teens Self-Reflection. (2018, February 18). Los Angeles Teen Therapist. https://losangesteentherapist.com/create-a-better-experience-of-life-through-self-reflection

TeensHealth. (2015). *Talking to Your Parents—or Other Adults (For Teens)*. Kidshealth. https://kidshealth.org/en/teens/talk-to-parents.html

Truett, S. (2018, July 2). *How to Say No Effectively: A Guide for Teenagers and Other People*. Relationship Builders. https://relationshipbuilders-lakeland.com/say-no-effectively-guide-teenagers-people/

Vavrichek, S. M. (2013, January 28). *How to Be Assertive While Keeping a Kind Heart*. PsychAlive. https://www.psychalive.org/how-to-be-assertive-while-keeping-a-kind-heart/

Violen, J. (2022, October 24). *Social Skills: Promoting Positive Behavior, Academic Success, and School Safety*. NASP Center. https://naspcenter.org/factsheets/social-skills/

Whyte, A. (2018, April 23). *How to Help Your Teen Set Healthy Dating Boundaries*. Evolve Treatment Centers. https://evolvetreatment.com/blog/healthy-dating-boundaries/

Made in United States
Troutdale, OR
11/08/2024

24585036R00095